Counting Down

I am at the pet shop.

I am looking at the birds.

I can see six birds.

6 birds

I am looking at the fish.

I can see five fish.

5 fish

I am looking at the mice.

I can see four mice.

4 mice

I am looking at the rabbits.

I can see three rabbits.

3 rabbits

I am looking at the puppies.

I can see two puppies.

2 puppies

I can see one kitten.

I **like** kittens.

1 kitten